Living Lines Are Never Straight

Barbara Orłowska-Westwood

Copyright © Barbara Orłowska-Westwood 2020

The moral rights of the author have been asserted.

All rights reserved. Except as permitted under the *Australian Copyright Act 1968* (for example, a fair dealing for the purposes of study, research, criticism or review), no part of this book may be reproduced, stored in a retrieval system, communicated or transmitted in any form or by any means without prior written permission.

Some of these poems, or their earlier versions were published in: *Beyond the Tree Brothers, Contrast, Earth Work, Fun Fact and Fiction, In the Attic of the Mind, Lights Falls, Seniors' Stories Vol 4, Poetry Australia (online), Port Pondering, The Australian Writer, Water – Waves – Words, Wind, Rain & Mud, World Enough, Writers' Ink, The Australian Writer, The Current, The Mozzie.*

Front cover artwork © Joorart.com

Typeset by BookPOD

ISBN: 978-0-6489700-0-2

A catalogue record for this book is available from the National Library of Australia

For my family and friends

Acknowledgements

I would like to thank my family and friends for their encouragement and support in the endeavour of publishing this book.

Thank you also to the members of the various writers' groups I have belonged to. You have been a part of the journey that brought me here. Especially, I would like to thank Trevor Code of the Deakin Literary Society for his advice and encouragement over the years, and to Brian Edwards of Deakin Literary Society for his recent editorial help.

A very special and heartful thank you to my daughter in-law, Joanna for her artwork for the cover and the paintings of blue wren, kangaroo and tree included in this book.

Contents

A Link	1
From the Depth	2
Living Lines are Never Straight	4
Djitti Djitti	5
Blue Wren	6
The Nest	8
Prisoners	10
Dreaming on Lord Howe Island	11
Shadows	12
Journey	14
Photograph of a Man on the Kindee Bridge	15
On My Walk	16
Boy in Blue Overalls	18
Summer Love	20

The Roads You Take	21
Blue-ringed Octopus	22
Waiting	24
Who am I	25
Mister C	26
The Ways of Progress	28
Grey Kangaroos	30
Sounds I Don't Hear	32
Kookaburra	33
Death and the Maiden	34
Panta Rei	38
Now	39
About the Author	40

A Link

Wet sheets of fog
wrap around me
cling to my skin
smell of seaweed
trapped in mist

warm breath
from the paddocks
sweeps the fog away

green rivers of scrub
flow towards the ocean
the dark shape of Wilsons Prom
cuts out of the horizon
a dinosaur
it rises from the ancient waters
and stretches
in the warmth of the sun

my life is
a blink of this monster's eye
flicker of a shooting star
a grain of sand
blown by the wind
yet I am a link
in a chain.

Walkerville, Victoria

From the Depth

In a liquid world of blues and greens
and the black silence of the depths
they live swaying
to the movement of wave and tide

The violence of storms
uproots them tears apart
the currents' turbulence
tosses and tumbles the fragments

Tides bring them to shore
bundles of ocean waste
drying out by the wind and sun
rotting buried in the sand

When you walk on the beach
look at them to see
their fragile crenulated beauty
nature's form so perfect
we only dream to create.

Living Lines are Never Straight

ECG lines rise and fall
draw an abstract form
    of being.

Behind a window
the camellia bud
yesterday
a green knot of inertia
today unfurls
    into a living cup.

In your sleep
the wall of your chest
rises and falls
on the tide of breath
a blue spider of veins
crawls on your hand.

Your body surrenders
to my fingers
in your pulse
I touch
    life's rhythm.

Djitti Djitti*

Your arrival startles me.
Black silk of your coat luminous
in the sun, the velvet camisole
a flash of white
when you dance.

Your movements are rapid, yet
at the end of every turn
you pose long enough
as if to say, look at me —
this side, and now that.

You dance and talk
high-pitched cadence
then stop, spread ebony wings,
your departure instant.
It leaves me wondering
if I have really met you.

the indigenous name of a Willy Wagtail comes from its call.

Blue Wren

At night I hear you
remember your hand
smoothing my hair

In the morning
you walk with me to the pond
to watch a diving duck
the wise steps
of the white-faced heron

On the way home
in a shop window
a porcelain Blue Wren
I stroke its folded wings
the cobalt breast is
tempting I don't buy it

I hear your voice *Why not?*
Today it gives you joy
tomorrow
won't be the same

© Joorart.com

The Nest

In the Spanish sun
the pylon shines
Danger! a black sign
white skull and crossbones.

On the pylon's arms
storks have built their nest.
From the woven rim
twigs and sticks prick the cloudless sky.
In the nest
two eggs waiting.
Klek...klek...klek...
stork's clattering call drifts
over olive groves, Spanish meadows
soaks into the heat
      stirs memories —
      the house, the pond, the barn,
      weeping willows.
      On the barn's roof
      an old wooden wheel.
      Storks knew it was for them.
      Every year after the thaw
      when soil freed of snow
      opened dark furrows to the sun,
      the storks returned
      circled over the barn calling
      ...klek...klek...klek...

The pylon's steel
crosses the blue Spanish sky
black wires carrying a lethal charge
beyond the horizon.

In the stork's nest
cradled by the pylon's arms
the first egg is hatching.

Prisoners

Over barbed wire I see
a mother and a child
they notice me   their feet
knead black dough of mud
their legs ready to run

*don't be afraid, I'm a friend
a mother like you*

my voice is muffled by wind and rain

*too cold, too wet in this paddock
wrong time to have a child
it needs the warmth of summer
as in your forebears' land*

The cow's big eyes glisten   blink
she turns towards the calf
oblivious of her genetic burden
she licks mud off the calf's head

Trapped
in a mat of black and white hide
the droplets of rain shine

Dreaming on Lord Howe Island

I clap, whistle.
From the bush
wild birds, the woodhens, come
cacao brown,
bars of black shining on wings,
eyes scanning the ground and me,
long beaks pick at scattered seeds.

Lost in evolution —
flight
and fear of predators.

For first settlers they were an easy catch.
Few survived the invasion.

While many young men
were shipped in body bags
from Vietnam
here someone bred
the woodhens, the wild things,
their threatened numbers grew.

I watch the birds
wandering on my path,
think about people
killed in Iraq, Afghanistan
I dream
one day we may live
without predators
like the woodhens.

Shadows

In a green cluster of melaleuca
blackbird sings a love song.
The sun is rising.
I walk, follow my shadow
black on the grey road.

I smile, remember childhood play
and lift my hands above my head
this shadow — a rabbit
ears straight
alert to any threatening sound.

Then I am a bird —
arms waving up and down
in a flight to nowhere.

I laugh, my fingers catch
the edge of my shorts, and head bent
I walk on tiptoe, Swan Lake music —
a ballerina whirls on gravel
stops, curtsies, waits for applause.

The music changes to Wagner.
My right hand thrusts upwards
I shout *Heil*
watching the hated pose
cast on the road.

I lean forward, hands over my face
the dark silhouette before me —
the Pietà of all mothers
cries in my shadow.

The blackbird calls again
magpies argue in the pines
and the sun at its zenith ends my play
forces all ghosts into hiding.

Journey

Uluru and Kata Tjuta
Pyramids of the Australian desert
Black Nomad's lighthouses
in the ocean of sand
the Sacred Rocks
born from the womb of Gondwanaland
keep their secrets locked
in ochre and ash
I wait wrapped in silence
thoughts run back thousands of years
join the spirits of those who were here

my body shivers   my soul
empty   an offering cup
ready to be filled
when the first touch of light
dilutes the darkness
the sun starts to paint the sky
the Rocks and I are born
to a new day

Photograph of a Man on the Kindee Bridge*

A man stands on the bridge
alone, his hair as grey
as the wood of the rail he leans on,
his face leathered
by sun, wind and rain,
above him trusses
criss-crossing the sky.
Like the bridge, he is the oldest
in his family — remembers
the bullock drays and pack horses.
No one has kept the record of his daily life;
no one knows how many people and carriages
passed over the bridge,
yet here
the man and the bridge,
integral parts
in the wheel of life.

Kindee Bridge, built in 1936, over the Hasting River is the oldest timber suspension bridge in NSW.

On My Walk

At the edge of a footpath
Dude, the surfer stands
made in discarded metal
bolts, nuts and wire.
His toes, a collection of teaspoons,
under his arm a surfboard
rusting like him.
He looks at me with glass eyes
blue from the sky.

Above him the maple's branch
is knobbed with new growth
ready to sprout.
Across the walking path
in a wooden cage,
the rubbish bins overflow
and caught on a dead gum's bark
a white plastic bag
waves in the breeze.

Away from road and people
in green haze of bush scented with honey
native bees swarm on a tea tree.
Banksia's new leaves washed in silver
tremble when a wattle bird
lands on a cone.
From a crack in the paver
melaleuca's green spear
turns to the sun.

Invaded by concrete, iron and plastic,
tamed by poison and axe,
bush grows back
with memory
of the light touch of black feet
the smell of a campfire, sound
of voices telling stories of life and death
in the language I cannot speak.

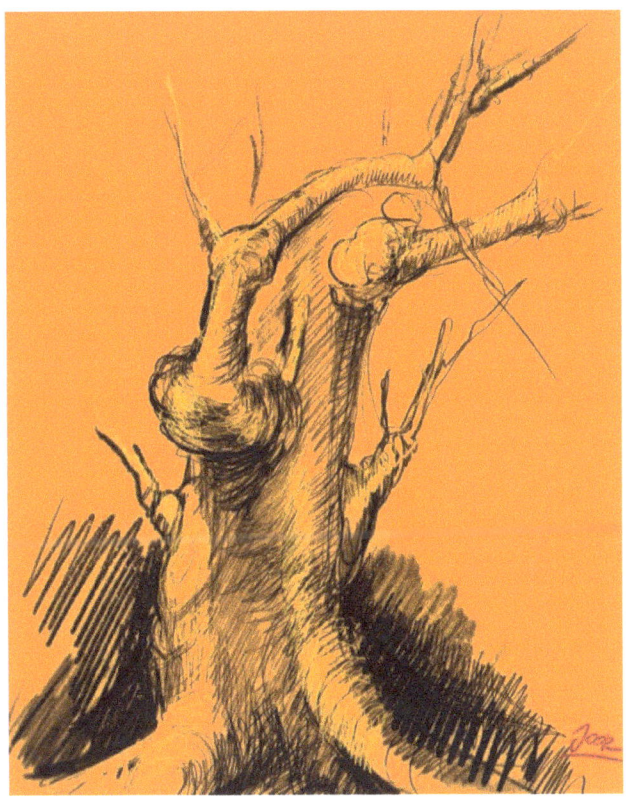

© Joorart.com

Boy in Blue Overalls

Flowers arranged by the artist
as he painted them on canvas —
orange and yellow splashed with red
pink mauve and purple amongst silvery foliage
blue mixed with white and cream.

On a square of lawn
an umbrella of paradise apple
the red balls of fruit
glimmer with moisture
Monet's house lost in mist.

Screened by the grey-green wall
of bamboo and weeping willows
his pond opens a dark eye
the willows' plaits
touch the water mirror.

Sun slants through the haze
fills in pink cups of water lilies
illuminates the green wooden boat
and blue overalls of the boy
in slow movements he scoops
the water lilies' spent flowers.

> *Does he think about Monet*
> *the artist's love of flowers*
> *harmony of colours*
> *the painter's obsession with the pond*
> *Japanese bridge and the water lilies?*

The boy finishes his task
ties the boat to a tree
moves out of the picture
back into his life
in the village of Giverny.

A breeze sweeps the mist away
unveils
Monet's pink and green house
on the pond
water lilies open new flowers.

Summer Love

It trailed over the rocks
survived the flood and drought
Acalypha reptans
all seasons tough,
not our love.

You taught me its other names.
Like the caress of a lover's hand
they arouse senses
inspire imagination
trigger memory.

Cola de Gatito — syllables
cascade off the tongue
vibrate, evoke a castanet's sound
scent of oranges and your body
on a hot Sevillian night.

Kitten Tail — brings back
softness of your skin
under my exploring fingers,
silkiness of your hair
brushing against my lips.

Trailing Chenille —
more music than words
a prelude's promise
we never discovered,
as a lilt of your voice
I stored in me.

The Roads You Take

Some are filled with light and colours
that seduce you from the first sight
their signs warn in time
of sharp turns and crossings
no broken stones   no potholes
under your feet
and with steady speed they carry you
to that special place

Sometimes your road
is shaded by doubts
uneasiness seeps from the shadows
no guide holds your hand when
the signs are hard to read
you watch every step
try not to trip and fall
detours test your strength
dim your hope
as the end like a mirage
moves further away

Then around a bend
a dirt path branches off
sun filters through the trees
a breeze rustles the leaves
a clearing opens up
invites you to walk in   rest
untangle confused thoughts
clear your vision
while above you in the blueness of sky
the eagle glides.

Blue-ringed Octopus*

words   not said
thoughts   not shared
things   not done

like old clothes
no use for them any more
I can't throw them away
give them to somebody
I'm not ready yet

I push them aside
I pack them
squash them into a suitcase
zip and leave it on the back shelf

it doesn't work
I can't forget
a blue-ringed octopus of guilt
takes shelter in me

during the day
its tentacles are pulled in
resting
it awakes at night
at that black hour
stretches
grows bigger and bigger
feeding on thoughts
of my regret

yet I live with the hope
that one endless night
it will stretch too much
break
and I will be free

*A small octopus of eastern Australia marked by blue banding on the tentacles and having a highly venomous bite. The Macquarie Dictionary.

Waiting

'The Ripple' on the Inverloch Inlet, 1908

The Inlet a plateau of grey slate
edged by the breakers' white froth

Water slaps at poles of the jetty
seagulls glide towards the shore

The Ripple rests, sails folded, covered
the masts sway to the wave's rhythm

They wait the breeze
flirts with the ribbons of the ladies' hats

plays with frills around smooth necks
slides to the deck on the folds of long skirts

He sits on the cockpit mouth organ to his lips
and plays for the girl he loves

Her eyes on the water in its mirror
she sees the other man's face

An old tune born in the country of their parents
drifts over the ocean soaks into hot sand

They wait for the change

Who am I

Born free
like sand or a word
like them often imprisoned

colourless   I may be black
as your guilt
or white as your past innocence

my odourless fluency can bring you
jasmine's fragrance
or a smell of sewer

shapeless I can take on any shape
I can wrap around you
with the softness of an evening breeze
but my force unleashed
will crush you without mercy

trapped
in nature's cycles
I move through many phases
but remain the same

Mister C

For Jeremi

Paw prints
marked your way to our porch
you slept there
torn ear oozing blood
on your shaggy coat
a wounded soldier
resting after battle

You heard me
alert you stood up
our eyes met
we liked what we saw

You allowed me
to clean your wounds
tape your ear
later I stroked your back
you purred

I didn't know your name
Ginger seemed too ordinary
I was certain in your previous life
you were a leopard
tracking prey in African jungle
or at least a gentlemen thief
sneaking into safes in the dark

We agreed on *Mister Cat*
you liked it and I felt
this name put you above
the common feline population
as I did my friend.

The Ways of Progress

Before the white missionaries
French invasion
and Mururoa nuclear testing
you lived off the land and the sea
the way your parents and grandparents did.
You had knowledge and skills
like the black hair and coffee-coloured skin
inherited from your ancestors.

In the long canoes you sailed faraway
the sun moon and stars your compass.
Clouds and birds the Pacific swell
and currents guided you.
Your bodies had muscles and strength
at home the women wove sarongs
planted taro and cooked in an earth oven.

Today lured by photos of turquoise lagoons
palm trees and girls in grass skirts
tourists flock to your islands
like nectar eating birds to tropical flowers.
They bring the hard currency you need to survive.
You welcome them with traditional songs
talk with pride about old customs
feed them coconuts papayas
show black pearls and shell necklaces
sold in shops and galleries by French traders.

Your bodies grow fat on supermarket food
your hands are weakened on steering wheels
oars and machetes are idle in your sheds.
In Papeete loudspeakers blast
American rap songs YouTube images
corrupt young minds promising the modern
paradise in Paris London and Montreal

While your ancestral land sinks
slowly and silently in the rising sea.

Tahiti 2018

Grey Kangaroos

I watch them
the mother and the child
separated by the wire fence.

The mother
on the side of the enclosure
hops back and forth alongside the wire
then sits next to it
her gaze on her child
across the fence.

He runs in small circles
stops opposite his mother
tries to scramble on the wire loops
resigns   circles again   comes back
sits facing her
their heads close.

I watch the pantomime
I do not need the words
their emotions palpable
reverberate in me.

Years ago
it was barbed wire and
the Iron Curtain.
You had stayed behind
when I left not knowing
if I would ever see you again
my mother.

Sounds I Don't Hear

On a fence wire
a microphone catches the hum
of a spider's weaving

two spires of grass brushing
must create a rustle
worker ants marching
on a tree trunk carrying their loads
groan and puff

sounds I don't hear
fill the blister of my silence

one day I might hear the scream
of a murdered butterfly

Kookaburra

When I come to the door
you flap your wings
leave a dry branch
of the distant tree
and fly straight to my feet.

Your landing is not perfect yet
but hunger
you know from your birth.
It has grown with your body.

I give you a scrap of meat
your beak shuts *clack*
on the treat. You talk to me
in your language. I tell you in mine
I like your visits.

Like flashlights they penetrate
the shadowy loneliness
of my isolation.

While a black bead of your eye
is watching me I wonder
if any thoughts are in your brain
and any understanding
of *yesterday* and *tomorrow*
or you live only
in *today*.

Death and the Maiden*

Classical Cape plays...
I read a flier pinned to the wall
of a sea-side café.
Schubert and Mahler
the music is tempting
Thought of a crowd
deters me.
I cannot wear the warning
'don't touch the wound'.
...for the victims...
the flier's last line
changes my mind.

Heat. Smoke haze.
It wraps around the gum trees,
the bushes, blurs the contours
of the Community Hall.
The smell of bushfire clings
to my skin, hair, clothes.
I carry it inside.

It is a country gathering.
The seats have no numbers —
children laughing
run between chairs.
In a corner two tables,
cups, an urn of boiling water
jars of coffee, tea bags,
plates of sweets
covered by tea towels.

Fanned on the ceiling
a spider a *Huntsman*,
the size of a child's hand.
You liked them —
let them live in your studio.
I smile at your shadow
and watch the spider.
The crowd fills the hall.

They walk onto the stage
in jeans and shorts.
On their black T-shirts
Classical Cape,
printed in red and blue.

The leader, a base player
carved solid as his instrument,
plays the tone.
A cacophony of string sounds
weaves into a murmur
rising from the floor,
breakers crashing on the rocks.

The face of the first violinist
is creased in concentration.
The third violin, a girl in her twenties,
has reddish hair, freckles.
Scottish blood, you would have said.
She smiles, winks at the cello man
who lifts his eyebrows, looks

at the girl, back to the cello
his bow moves on the strings.

Death and the Maiden
Schubert's music flows.
Stay away. Oh, stay away
plead the violins,
you will sleep softly in my arms
lure the violas and cellos
go fierce death, go
the violins' cry suppressed
by the accordance of the bass
and cellos.
The rhythm changes to a frenzy
then ebbs into silence.

That Saturday
you had no time to plead,
death didn't lure you
it struck in fury of the fire storm
leaving a mute moonscape,
ashes,
the embers glowing through the night.

They play again —
the second movement, allegro.
Sound fills the hall
spills through the wall cracks
into the bush.

The music flows.
In the distance a kookaburra laughs.
The child next to me smiles
and I smile remembering
the crooked house
you built for the red rosellas.

On the way out
I looked at the spider.
It hadn't changed position,
was it listening?

It must like the music
I can hear you saying.

Schubert's String Quartet No.14 "Death and The Maiden"

Panta Rei

Everything is in a state of continuous change.
Heraclites of Ephesus c.500 BC

Oak and maple leaves
turned rust-colour
and shrivelled
in the chill of night

In an empty park
a girl walks into the sun
her head touches the sky
her heart still full of spring
unaware of winter
which like a cat
sneaks from behind the corner

Now

I watch the magpies feeding
on worms in our garden.
My fingers hover
over the laptop's keys
but the poems that circle in my head
like a flock of crows
cry requiem
for the people and things
of *yesterdays*. Yet
it is *today*
and every moment
is the last.
I shouldn't waste it
mourning the past.
I need to chase the dark thoughts
from my mind
like I chase crows
from my gum tree
and let the lorikeets and galahs
flow in
with ideas for poems
vibrant with colours
pulsating with energy
calling like those birds
in a loud voice
the joy of being
now

About the Author

Barbara Orlowska-Westwood was born in Poland and migrated to Australia in 1979. A physician, now retired, she worked in her profession in both countries. In retirement, she enjoys writing poetry and prose and her writing has been published in Australia, Poland and America. A chapbook of her poetry *Firing Neurons* was published by PressPress in 2010.

www.ingramcontent.com/pod-product-compliance
Lightning Source LLC
Chambersburg PA
CBHW040244010526
44107CB00065B/2866